LoveWorld Publishing

Prophecy: Understanding The Power That Controls Your Future

ISBN 978-37865-3-9

First Printing 2005, Second Printing 2007

All scripture quotations are taken from the *King James Version* of the Bible unless otherwise indicated.

BELIEVERS' LOVEWORLD INC.
aka Christ Embassy

UNITED KINGDOM:
Christ Embassy Int'l Office
363 Springfield Road, Chelmsford
Essex, CM2 6AW
Tel:+44 1245 490 234

USA:
Christ Embassy Int'l Office,
2616 Texas Dr A,
Irving, Texas 75062
Tel: +1-972-255-1787

SOUTH AFRICA:
Cnr. Harley and Hendrik Vewoerd
Randburg, Gauteng.
South Africa.
Tel: +27-72-241 7332

NIGERIA:
P.O. Box 1356, Ikeja, Lagos.
Tel:+234-802 3324 188,
+234-805 2464 131,
+234-1-892 5724

email: cec@christembassy.org
website: www.christembassy.org

CONTENTS

INTRODUCTION

A People of Prophecy

God's people are a people of prophecy. God called us out by prophecy, builds us up by prophecy, sends us out by prophecy, and blesses us so much through prophecy. This is why prophecy is such an important subject in the Kingdom of God and in this book I'll be teaching you how prophecy affects your life—indeed how it has affected your life up to this point and is already shaping your future.

I'll also be showing you how you can take

advantage of this powerful gift of prophecy given you by God to create the kind of future you want to have.

You'd learn in this timely book that your future is not just in your hands but in your mouth, and it's up to you to speak it into existence. You'll discover that your mouth has been fashioned by God as the compass of your life; you can use it rightly and arrive in the future of your dreams.

I hope that not only would you read but you'd also receive into your spirit all I share with you in this book about prophecy, and begin to consciously and consistently order the course of your life and your future in the direction you want through the power of prophecy.

Chapter One

FORETELLING AND FORTH-TELLING

I said in my introduction that God's people are a people of prophecy. We are made by prophecy, but a lot of us don't understand what prophecy really is.

When I say we are a people of prophecy, it's the same as saying we are a people of promise. In Romans 9:8 Paul said, *"They which are the children of the flesh, these are not the children of God: but the children of the promise are counted for the seed."*

What the promise refers to here is the Word. Now,

the prophecy I'm talking about is the prophecy of the Word, and it has a two-fold application: foretelling and forth-telling.

"Foretelling" is not the same as fortune-telling, palm-reading, star-gazing, crystal-gazing or zodiac sign reading. To foretell, according to the scriptures, means to tell ahead of time things in the mind of God concerning a person or people, places or events.

"Forth-telling," on the other hand, means to speak forth, tell out or tell forward what is in the mind of God. It's the declaration of events in the mind of God or the declaration of a particular Word from God to an individual, people, place, or event for a particular time.

Prophecy, therefore, is in two categories. The one category is the ministry of a prophet, while the other is the use of the gift of prophecy, which is given to any believer who has the Holy Spirit, as the Spirit wills.

The Gift of Prophecy

Paul talks in detail about the gift of prophecy (and the prophetic office) in 1 Corinthians 14. In verse 29, he said, *"Let the prophets speak two or three, and let the other judge."* He also said, "If any thing be *revealed* to another that sitteth by, let the first hold his peace," that is, "Let him finish speaking."

This is talking about prophets specifically, but in the next verse, he says, *"For ye may all prophesy one by one, that all may learn, and all may be comforted"* (1 Corinthians 14:31). He let us know that everyone of us can prophesy. But everybody who prophesies is not necessarily a prophet. To be a prophet, you have to be called into that ministry office.

However, you can be given a prophetic utterance without being a prophet. That's up to God; anybody can speak for Him when He enables them to. After all, He made a dumb ass speak.

The gift of prophecy is for exhortation, comfort, and edification. Unlike the operation of the prophetic office, this utterance doesn't necessarily have to do with a revelation or have a revelation behind it.

In Romans 12:6 Paul says, *"Having then **gifts** differing according to the grace that is given to us,* ***whether prophecy, let us prophesy according to the proportion of faith;"***

This means the one who prophesies should speak according to the proportion of faith. This kind of prophecy is a faith utterance; it's quite different from the revelation-based utterance of a prophet.

Another child of God can make a prophetic utterance to you and say, "Thus saith the Holy Ghost, I am with you; therefore, be strong my child." He doesn't have to have a vision or a special revelation of your situation to do that. But he has a Word of faith, and by faith, he declares that Word unto you. And while he's doing that, he doesn't have to act like something has come over him and he doesn't know what's happening to him.

In using the gift of prophecy, you speak according to the proportion of faith. That's why a minister of God can tell you, "You're going to receive a special blessing this week!" Then he realizes he uttered the word by faith, and says, "That's a prophecy; you're going to get it!" He didn't need to have any special revelation to say that.

The Prophetic Office

The prophetic office is however quite different from the gift of prophecy. To operate in the prophetic office, one has to be called of God into that office as a prophet.

This is the office Paul referred to in Ephesians 4:11: *"And he gave some, apostles; and some,* ***prophets;*** *and some, evangelists; and some, pastors and teachers;"*

The office of the prophet is one of the five-fold ministry gifts God has set forth in the Church for the perfecting of the saints, for the work of the ministry, and for the edifying of the body of Christ" (Ephesians 4:12).

Prophets have revelations, signs, and wonders. They are men who hear from God and speak forth what they've heard, and it comes to pass.

Back in the Old Testament, if someone consistently spoke words that were anointed by the Spirit of God, and they came to pass, they knew him to be a prophet. They recognised that only those sent by the

Spirit of God could do such things.

The prophetic office is however not the focus of this book. Instead, we'll be dealing with that manifestation of the Spirit of God in our lives as believers whereby we speak words of faith and power.

Words of Power

This is another very important point about prophecy: it is **a word of power spoken to either foretell events or bring forth God's Word into a situation in the now.**

To prophesy, therefore, would mean to speak words of power, words filled with the ability of God to cause changes and make things to happen.

Whether you're foretelling events or speaking forth the mind of God concerning issues, persons, places or events, as long as it comes to pass, it's a word of power.

To be able to tell things ahead of time or tell forth something that's in the mind of God, and for those things to come to pass, there must be ability in your words, there must be power to back them up and make them work.

This means such words must contain a divine ability to make them come to pass. They must be from God and be inspired by His Spirit. That's what prophecy is, because you spoke ahead of time and your words came to pass!

PROPHECY IN THE LAST DAYS

In Joel chapter 2 and verse 28, Prophet Joel prophesied the mind of God concerning God's people in these last days:

> *"And it shall come to pass afterward, that I will pour out my spirit upon all flesh; and your sons and your daughters shall prophesy, your old men shall dream dreams, your young men shall see visions: And also upon the servants and upon the handmaids in those days will I pour out my spirit."*

Something very significant happened on the day of Pentecost in Acts 2 that marked the fulfilment of this prophecy. 120 disciples of Jesus were gathered together in one accord and suddenly the Holy Ghost came upon them and filled them. Then they started speaking in tongues and prophesying.

They sang, danced, swayed, and staggered drunkenly all over the temple court where they were gathered. They made so much noise that many of those who heard them mocked, saying they were drunk.

Then Peter spoke up for the group and told the crowd, *"Ye men of Judaea, and all ye that dwell at Jerusalem, be this known unto you, and hearken to my words: For these are not drunken, as ye suppose, seeing it is but the third hour of the day. But this is that which was spoken by the prophet Joel; And it shall come to pass in the last days, saith God, I will pour out of my Spirit upon all flesh: and your sons and your daughters shall prophesy, and your young men shall see visions, and your old men shall dream dreams: And on my servants and on my handmaidens I will pour out in those days of my Spirit; and they shall prophesy:"* (Acts 2:16).

God promised that He would pour out His Spirit upon all flesh and they shall prophesy. That promise has since been fulfilled, and the same Holy Spirit that was poured upon those 120 early disciples of Jesus has been poured upon us today to enable us prophesy.

And when we prophesy, we're speaking words of power that affect our bodies, families, and finances; words that order the course of our lives today and shape our future.

Chapter Two

THE VALLEY OF DRY BONES

Throughout the Scriptures, God reveals to us just how important and powerful prophecy is. One of such portions of Scripture is found in the thirty-seventh chapter of the book of Ezekiel:

> *"The hand of the Lord was upon me, and carried me out in the spirit of the Lord, and set me down in the midst of the valley which was full of bones, And caused me to pass by them round about: and, behold,*

> *there were very many in the open valley; and, lo, they were very dry. And he said unto me, Son of man, can these bones live? And I answered, O Lord God, thou knowest"* (Ezekiel 37:1-3).

God took Ezekiel to a valley full of dry bones. There were dead men's bones everywhere, as far as the eyes could see all over that open valley. And in Ezekiel's description, the bones were very dry indeed.

Then God asked Ezekiel a pointed question, "Can these bones live?" In other words, "Can things change here?"

Ezekiel looked around and probably thought to himself, *"It looks really bad here, I doubt that they can,"* but he replied, "Well, Lord, Thou knowest!"

He was telling God in other words, "You only know if they can live or not. It's up to you to decide! If you want them to live, they'll live. If you don't want them to live, they won't." He threw the ball right back in God's court!

The Lord's response was very instructive. He told

him, "It's not up to Me, Ezekiel; it's up to you to do something about these bones and see to it that they live!"

God then told him what to do. He said,

> *"...Prophesy upon these bones, and say unto them, O ye dry bones, hear the word of the Lord. Thus saith the Lord God unto these bones; Behold, I will cause breath to enter into you, and ye shall live:"*
>
> (Ezekiel 37:4-6).

God told Ezekiel to prophesy to the bones and tell them, "Oh ye dry bones, hear the Word of the Lord. God's going to cause breath to come into you and you shall live!"

God was teaching Ezekiel how to change things through prophecy, and He taught him exactly what to say in his prophecy.

> *"And I will lay sinews upon you, and will bring up flesh upon you, and cover you with skin, and put breath in you, and ye shall live; and ye shall know that I am the Lord."*

Ezekiel saw that as he prophesied to the dry bones, something began to happen, so he prophesied some more as God taught him and gave him words to speak:

> *"So I prophesied as I was commanded: and as I prophesied, there was a noise, and behold a shaking, and the bones came together, bone to his bone"* (Verses 6 & 7).

Can you picture this! Imagine this huge heap of bones with each bone shifting around, searching for its members, and joining together until they all formed human skeletons! What a great noise they must have made in that open valley!

I like the next verse even more:

> *"And when I beheld, lo, the sinews and the flesh came up upon them, and the skin covered them above: but there was no breath in them."*

At this time they were no longer dry skeletons. As Ezekiel prophesied the Word of the Lord, the skeletons were covered with muscles, tendons, ligaments, and skin, and now looked like corpses spread all over the valley.

Ezekiel continued to prophesy as the Lord instructed him to:

> *"Then said he unto me, Prophesy unto the wind, prophesy, son of man, and say to the wind, Thus saith the Lord God; Come from the four winds, O breath, and breathe upon these slain, that they may live"*
>
> (Ezekiel 37:9).

Understand what God is talking about here. He's letting you know you can prophesy to the things you want changed. You can also prophesy to God Himself.

Observe what He said: "Prophesy unto the wind." That wind represents the Spirit of God. He said, *"Come from the four winds, O breath."* The original Hebrew word rendered "breath" here can also be stretched to mean "breath of life," which is synonymous with the Holy Spirit of God.

> Ezekiel 37:10: *"So I prophesied as he commanded me, and the breath (of life) came into them, and they lived, and stood up upon their feet, an exceeding great army."*

Prophesy To The Car!

Ezekiel prophesied to the dry bones of dead men and it worked! Those dried up, bleached-white bones received life, flesh, muscles, and skin and stood up a mighty army, brimming with life in that open valley.

This marvellous account reminds me of an incident back in 1984. My dad had several cars, but after a while, they started packing up one after the other. I went home on holiday from school one day to discover that none of the cars was working. So I said to him, "Dad, you've got to talk to these cars! Prophesy to them!"

Talk to the car? He'd never heard that before! At the beginning, he found it hard to believe, and for some time, he looked at me suspiciously, wondering where I got such information from. But each time I was home from school, I would talk about these things and share with him how to prophesy to his car.

He finally believed and started putting it to work, and before long the results came. One after the other, his cars received life and got back on the road.

Yes! You can talk to your car, house, job, business, money, or bank account, and whatever was dead or dying will receive life and be active again.

PROPHECY: THE SPOKEN, REVEALED WORD OF GOD

Prophecy is the spoken Word of God; it is the revealed Word of God by which He leads and guides His people. The man who prophesies speaks with the ability of God's Spirit.

When God said in Joel 2:28, "Your sons and your daughters shall prophesy," He meant that everybody in the Kingdom will have this ability of God to prophesy, to speak forth God's Word and cause it to come to pass.

We'll all be able to bring about changes that will affect our lives and the lives of others around us positively.

What power, what great knowledge this is! How exciting to know you're not at the mercy of life's circumstances. If the life you have is not appealing to you, you can change it. You can control your destiny by the power of God made available to you through prophecy!

Some people don't believe this but it doesn't matter whether they believe it or not. God didn't say they *must* believe it; He says the one who believes is blessed but the one who doesn't is damned. So the choice is yours to make.

If you say you believe, what have you done so far with what you've believed? If you haven't done much with it, what you need to do is believe even more and make up your mind to put what you believe to work.

God says to us, *"It shall come to pass in the last days that I will pour out of my Spirit upon all flesh: and your sons and your daughters shall prophesy, your young men shall see visions and your old men shall dream dreams."*

This is not talking about seeing scary things or having nightmares. He tells you the kind of things you should see: "*the young men shall* ***see visions****, and your old men shall* ***dream dreams.***" These are the things you ought to be seeing–visions and dreams of God inspired in you by the Holy Spirit–and you see them with the eyes of your spirit.

When the Spirit is poured out, you'll prophesy. I want to let you know that doesn't mean you'll say, "Thus saith the Lord, Jesus is coming again!" Of course, Jesus is coming again, but that's not going to affect your job, your family or your finances in the now! There's more to prophecy than that.

When God said you'll prophesy, He meant you'll speak words of power and revelation, and you'll cause things to come to pass through your words. This is how the power of God works with dynamic ability to cause changes in our lives and circumstances.

Understand this and it will change your whole world. I started doing this several years ago and I still do it today. I'd pray and prophesy and pull out my notepad and write down all those prophecies. I've followed those notes for years and the things I wrote down have come to pass just like God said they would.

One time, some people were looking at some of the prophecies I wrote down, and I said to them, "That's as sure as the Scriptures, because it's the same Spirit." Now, of course, your prophecy should never contradict the Word of God. If it's not based on the Word, you might as well throw it in the trash! But most of those prophecies have come to pass and we are living right in the manifestation of the others now. Praise God!

Prophecy Edifies The Church

"For he that speaketh in an unknown tongue speaketh not unto men, but unto God: for no man understandeth him; howbeit in the spirit he speaketh mysteries. But he that prophesieth speaketh unto men to edification, and exhortation, and comfort"

(1 Corinthians 14:2-3).

Paul didn't say, *"he that prophesieth speaketh unto men to witch-hunt, catch sinners, or act as spiritual detectives."* Have you ever come across such self-styled, self-appointed "spiritual gauges" in God's house? I've met some of them; they'll tell you, "When my left hand gets hot, that means there's a sinner close to my left."

I was in the service in a certain church many years ago. The pastor of the church had received a letter from their denominational headquarters transferring him to another city to pastor another branch of their ministry.

Some of the members, of course, didn't want the pastor to go, which was not unusual. But something happened in that service that was wrong. The new pastor had come to resume and some of the church members began to prophesy against him. The worship segment was disrupted as several members interrupted the worship and prophesied that the transfer was wrong. The result was chaos in the church. Some of the members became riotous and decided the church will not continue if the now former pastor was transferred and the new one brought in.

The church was divided, as some supported the transfer while others didn't. I remember some of the protesters went outside the building and pulled the signboard of the church off the ground. The prophecies had ruined the service, and now threatened to ruin the church. Such prophecies are definitely not from God. His prophecies are for edification, exhortation, and comfort (1 Corinthians 14:3).

Prophecy and Tongues

In verses 3 and 4 of 1 Corinthians 14, Paul went on to say *"He that prophesieth speaketh unto men to edification, and exhortation, and comfort. He that speaketh in an unknown tongue edifieth himself; but he that prophesieth edifieth the church."*

When you speak in other tongues you edify your spirit. It doesn't edify others because they don't know what you're talking about. Paul actually said later in verse 11, *"Therefore if I know not the meaning of the voice, I shall be unto him that speaketh a barbarian, and he that speaketh shall be a barbarian unto me."*

However, the one who prophesies edifies the Church, and Paul encourages us in verse 12: *"Even so ye, forasmuch as ye are zealous of spiritual gifts, seek that ye may excel to the* ***edifying of the church****."*

Paul was saying in other words, "Seek that you may excel in prophecy," because the one who prophesies edifies the Church. Prophecy is very important; it edifies the Church. And if it edifies the Church, it will edify you because you're a part of the Church.

When you're prophesying, you're doing it in your understanding, and by that I mean you're speaking in a language you understand. That way, those listening to you are blessed because they can hear you and understand what you're saying. You're blessed too because you also understand what you're saying.

Now, the Bible says if you speak in other tongues (that is, if you have a message from God to His people in other tongues), you can pray and ask Him for the interpretation, because when you speak in other tongues and also interpret, that equals prophecy. God's people will then be blessed by your words of prophecy.

How important prophecy is! God said, *"In the last*

days I will pour out my Spirit on all flesh and your sons and daughters shall prophesy." This means they can change things with their mouths. Remember, I said prophecy means that you're foretelling (telling ahead of time what is going to happen) and then forth-telling (revealing or declaring the Word, mind, or purpose of God concerning a person or people, places or events).

It's absolutely imperative that you speak forth the Word concerning you, because until you do, it will have no power and it won't work!

It's like having a Bible in your hands; it's the written Word of God and it contains the gospel that saves, but until you tell it forth, it will have no power to save anybody.

You can't put your Bible on a sick person's head and expect him to get healed; you've got to declare, "Be healed in Jesus' Name." The Name of Jesus has also been given to us, but until you use that Name in faith, recognizing the authority in it that has been vested in you, the sick won't be healed and the demons won't flee. You've got to speak forth in the Name of Jesus. God's

Word in your life becomes efficacious as you declare it by prophecy.

Chapter Three

"YE ARE GODS!"

In Psalm 82, the Psalmist gives a very touching narrative of the course of men's lives when they lack the knowledge and understanding of God's will concerning them:

> *"God standeth in the congregation of the mighty; he judgeth among the gods. How long will ye judge unjustly, and accept the persons of the wicked? Selah. Defend the poor and fatherless: do justice to the af-*

> *flicted and needy. Deliver the poor and needy: rid them out of the hand of the wicked. They know not, neither will they understand; they walk on in darkness:* ***all the foundations of the earth are out of course.*** *I have said, Ye are gods; and all of you are children of the most High. But ye shall die like men, and fall like one of the princes. Arise, O God, judge the earth: for thou shalt inherit all nations."*

Understand what's going on here. Everything is unstable and out of course for these people. Things aren't working out right for them. They walk in darkness and the foundations of their lives are out of course. Worse still, they die like mere men and fall like earthly princes. Yet, we're told they are gods and all of them are children of the Most High. Why then do these things happen to them?

The answer is right there in verse 5: *"They know not, neither will they understand; they walk on in darkness...."* Men walk on in darkness, sickness, poverty, depression, unhappiness because don't know the way of the Spirit. They walk according to their sensory perception.

The Psalmist said, "they know not, neither will they understand"(Psalm 82:5); that's why they walk on in darkness and all the foundations of their world are out of course. God has laid the foundations and set the right course but men have changed them. Now their health foundation, business foundation, prosperity foundation, and all other foundations of their lives are unstable. But when God made all things, He founded them rightly and said, "It is very good."

So how come things aren't very good for some folks? Somebody looks at his future and says, "It's very bleak. It doesn't look good at all." He goes for a medical check up, and the doctor's prognosis is not good. He looks at his finances, and they're not good. What's happening to him?

It's because he doesn't know and has also refused to acquire understanding. That's why all the foundations of his world are out of course. God is not responsible for his problems.

God said, "I have said, Ye are gods." I want you to observe God's language here very closely. He didn't say, "*I say*, Ye are gods" but "I *have said,* ye are gods," meaning that He had told them who they were before, but they weren't listening.

However, when you're born again, He fills you with His Spirit and says to you, "Go and prophesy!" Then you can go ahead and confess who He's made you to be and what He's made available for you. You can say, "Lord Jesus, thank You! I know who I am; I am the King's kid. Therefore, I'll never be poor; I'll never be a failure; I'm a success; I'm a victor; I live in health, in the Name of Jesus!

There are those who don't believe. I don't have to look far to know who believes and who doesn't. Their lives show it. They live as victims of the system and the circumstances they find themselves. But for those of us who believe and have put it to work, we've discovered that our words come to pass.

The Bible says in **Ecclesiastes 8:4**: *"Where the word of a king is, there is power: and who may say unto him, What doest thou?"* Also remember John's words in

Revelations 5:10: *"And (Jesus) hast made us unto our God* ***kings*** *and priests: and we shall reign on the earth."* Our words have power; for we are kings and shall reign on the earth. Prophecy is a word of power spoken by one who's anointed of the Holy Spirit. Recognize this when you speak and your words will come to pass.

Chapter Four

YOU ARE THE PROPHET OF YOUR LIFE!

The Lord carried Ezekiel away in the Spirit to a valley which was full of dry bones. To Ezekiel, it was a hopeless situation.

Then the Lord asked him, "Can these bones live?" and he replied, "Lord, it's up to You." That's what we say to God sometimes when He asks us, "Can these things change?" We tell Him it's up to Him; if He wants things to change, they will, and if He doesn't, they'll remain the way they are. That's not true. If God were running everything and running everyone's life the way many of us think He is, then He certainly has everything in a mess. He's not running everything. The fact is that many people are running their own lives, and many others have handed the reins of their lives to the devil.

I heard about a man who was in a church meeting where the preacher was explaining to the people how they were responsible for the things happening in their lives. This man got up and angrily stomped out of the church. Someone asked him at the door why he was leaving and he said he didn't agree with the preacher. He was angry at the preacher for "trying to blame us for everything."

You see, people would rather lay the blame of their misfortunes on God. Once they don't understand why certain things are happening, you'll hear them say, "God works in mysterious ways, His wonders to perform." "We can't tell how God is going to move. He might choose to bless us someday."

God doesn't run anybody's life that way. If you study the Bible, you'll see that He has actually given us the power to influence our destiny, to control our future and whatever happens to us in life. You can actually affect your life, your future, and your own world. So whatever becomes of you is really up to you!

Kenneth Hagin Tells A Story

Kenneth Hagin tells the story of a woman who came to him for prayer for her 15 year-old son. When she asked him to pray, he told her his prayer wasn't going to do any good.

She asked him why, and he said to her, "If I pray for your son, you'll nullify it because you're always telling him he'll end up in the penitentiary and never amount to any thing. So it won't do any good for me to pray for him." In desperation, she asked, "What am I going to do now?" He then counselled her: "Stop worrying about him getting saved and start thanking God for his life. Thank God for taking care of him wherever he is, instead of worrying something terrible is going to happen to him. They may bring him home to you dead that way! Thank

God for him and declare, "Lord, I cast all my cares on you because you care for me and you care for my son. Wherever he is, he's right in your hands."

She began to learn that, and several months later she came back and said it worked. Her son was born-again, and just the same way he was all-out for the devil, he became all-out for God, Hallelujah!

Say It, See It, And You've Got It!

David Yongi Cho also tells a similar story of a woman who came to him and said, "Pastor, help me! My daughter is making the whole family sick. She's such a wayward, evil sinner. I've prayed to God and nothing has changed..." she ranted on and on.

"Woman, you're in greater trouble than your daughter!" Pastor Cho chided. Can't you just for a moment see a beautiful, successful, honest, decent daughter?"

"Oh no, Pastor. You don't know my daughter" she

said. "She's wayward. Right now as we speak, she's in a hotel somewhere with some man. We're all embarrassed; we don't know what to do with her."

"Don't talk like that!" Pastor Cho rebuked her again.

"I can't help it," she replied.

"Well, as long as you see your daughter like that, that's the way she's going to be. But you can decide to see her coming back home born again, filled with God's Spirit, a wonderful Christian," he told her.

"Oh, that would be wonderful," she said.

Then he told her he wasn't going to pray until she started seeing that, and instructed her to write this down and declare it everyday:

"My daughter is born-again. She's filled with the Spirit. She's a wonderful Christian and she's coming back home."

She took the slip home and read it out loud to herself again and again everyday until she got so filled with it, she began to see it.

Several weeks later, she came back to Pastor Cho and announced excitedly, "Pastor, my daughter is a wonderful Christian. She's saved; she's full of the Holy Spirit and she's coming back home. Oh, I just can't wait, thank you Lord!" She was filled with such joy, they had a hard time calming her.

"Now we can pray!" Pastor Cho said and he prayed a simple prayer of agreement with her.

A few days later, very late in the night, there was a knock on the door. She opened the door and there stood her daughter! She told her mother she didn't know what came over her in the hotel room, but she got rid of the man and came right home, and now she wanted Jesus in her heart.

She was born-again and filled with the Holy Ghost that night. Glory to God! Don't tell me it doesn't work. You can prophesy your future. Your future is right in your mouth!

"Go Forth and Prosper!"

Some years ago, a young man came to me lamenting that everything he'd ever done had failed.

I asked if he'd been born again for long and he

said he'd been a Christian several years.

I sat him down, opened my Bible and showed him a few scriptures. Then I asked him, "See here, who's responsible for riches?"

"God," he said.

"How about wealth?

"God."

"Strength?"

"It's God."

"Who makes men great?"

"God," he answered again.

Then I said to him, "In the Name of Jesus, go forth and prosper and fail no more!"

He began to prosper in all things from that day forth!

You've got to understand, however, that it's all in the Word. You don't have any reason to fail; that has been ruled out of your life. You've got to have that as your spiritual mentality, not just something you assent to in your head. You must receive it as a revelation in your spirit.

There's a new kind of thinking for the child of God,

and the only way you get it is not by praying to God to give it to you, but by studying the Word of God. The Word will change your thinking to line up with God's thinking.

For example, I can't get healed from malaria or from any disease for that matter. Why do I say that? It's because I can't have it in the first place. The very fact that I'm claiming healing from malaria means I've agreed that I was infected with it. But I know I can't have an infection because I've been declaring it for years and it's been that way. You can declare the same and live a disease-free and disease-proof life.

Say this: ***"I'm going from health to health; from success to success; from strength to strength. I'm growing in knowledge, in understanding, and in wisdom. The ability of God is at work in me. I can never be a failure, I am a success. The Hand of God is upon my life, I'm moving forward and making progress. The strength of God is in me. The spirit of might is at work in me. I look ahead with great expectation because I know I have a great future. Thank You Lord Jesus!"***

Don't Curse; Prophesy!

You can speak God's Word concerning you and the things you're involved with. You can also speak God's Word concerning the Church. I tell God's people not to curse or say the wrong things about the Church. You're a part of the Church and whatever you say about the Church will reflect on you and affect your life.

Don't say the Church is weak and in need of revival. No! Why don't you prophesy instead that the power of God is going to move in the Church? Talk about the wind of God's Spirit that's going to blow through the Church, because He said, "In the last days, I will pour out my Spirit upon all flesh." You ought to declare that things are working out right in the Church because the Spirit of God is moving in her!"

Look at Israel; they messed up and blew it so many times, but the prophets would come and say things like, "A remnant shall be delivered." Always, they were inspired by God to prophesy right concerning Israel, because He knew the power to keep the people in the Kingdom and in line with His will rested in prophecy.

God said through Jeremiah the prophet, *"Refrain thy voice from weeping, and thine eyes from tears: for thy work shall be rewarded...and they shall come again from the land of the enemy ...there is hope in thine end... thy children shall come again to their own border"* (Jeremiah 31:16-17). That's what God said about the children of Israel, and that's what He's saying today concerning the Church.

Prophesy About Your Life and Your Future!

Peter, reiterating Joel's prophecy, said, *"And it shall come to pass in the last days, saith God, I will pour out of my Spirit upon all flesh: and your sons and your daughters shall prophesy, and your young men shall see visions, and your old men shall dream dreams: And on my servants and on my handmaidens I will pour out in those days of my Spirit; and they shall prophesy:"*

This ought to let you know that as a child of God, filled with the Holy Spirit, you have received the enablement to speak words of power. Remember again that one of the two aspects of prophecy is speaking FORTH the Word of God. As you speak forth the Word concerning you under the anointing, you are prophesying upon your life, and what you say is what you get.

You're going to have to learn to prophesy to your life and your future. You need to know this: **Your future is in your mouth**. You're fully responsible for your future, nobody else is. There are no limits to what you can imagine and make out of your life. That's because God has set the world (that means all of eternity) in the hearts of men (Ecclesiastes 3:11).

Every time you speak about your life or your future, you're actually prophesying. The only problem is you may have been a "false prophet." Romans 3:4 says, *"God forbid: yea, let God be true, but every man a liar; as it is written, That thou mightest be justified in thy sayings, and mightest overcome when thou art judged."* So if God has said something about you and you've been saying something else, then you've been lying. You've made yourself a false prophet over your own life!

instance, if God has said you're a new creature (2 Corinthians 5:17) and your path is as the shining light, that shines brighter and brighter unto the perfect day (Proverbs 4:18), and you say, *"I don't feel like one, I don't think I am. I think I need to be born again all over again. I don't understand my life anymore. My future looks so bleak and hopeless. I'm not living; I'm merely existing,"* then you're lying. You've made yourself into a false prophet.

I wish you would understand the power of prophecy. Did you know that from that "zero point" where you are, you can chart a new course for your life and determine your future through words of power?

Yes, you can! You can prophesy about your life and declare the future you want to have from now.

You might feel like the most neglected person on the face of the earth. You may be all alone in your room, crying because you feel like everything has gone bad. In the midst of your tears, you can begin to prophesy to yourself and say, "Thus saith the Lord unto you, I am with you, son. I am your Shepherd; therefore, you shall not want!"

You may be in pain, but you call your name and declare to yourself, "You're coming out of this pain in the Name of Jesus. I prophesy to you, you're coming out of this!" Hallelujah!

Many times we're waiting on somebody to utter a word for us to be blessed, but we're the children of the Word, and the Word concerning us has already been given. You don't have to wait for someone else to come and declare that to you. You can tell it to yourself.

That's the way I've been talking all these years and that is all I have experienced, no ups-and-downs, just the upward and forward life. Glory to God!

Chapter five

CHART YOUR COURSE WITH YOUR MOUTH

The Bible says the captain of a great ship controls that massive ship with a small helm, and compares that helm to the tongue. It says though the tongue is a little member, it boasts great things (James 3:5). Put your tongue to work and let it bring forth great things in your life.

As small as your tongue is, it's the most powerful member in your body. Your tongue can take you either to heaven or to hell. It can make you rich or poor, put new clothes on your back or dress you up in rags. It all depends on how you use it.

You see people in the streets, homeless and destitute—their tongues kept them there. It doesn't matter how you got into the situation you're in, you don't have to stay there. Your tongue can stop you from receiving what you ought to have or bring it to you. It all depends on how you use it.

Now if you don't use your tongue at all, don't think nothing will happen, something will still result from that. You know there's no such thing as a clean piece of farmland waiting to be cultivated. If the farmer doesn't sow something in the farm, it would grow something by itself, something unwanted—weeds.

So when you say, "Whatever will be, will be," that's like you saying, "Well, I've cleared this piece of land, whatever can grow there should grow." You can be sure what's going to grow there won't be nice.

You can use your tongue to programme yourself for a successful, tremendous life or for a life full of grief and regrets.

The Manufacturer, The Manual and the Machine

There are several parts in a camera; some of them may be quite complex, but when you have the manual, you can learn about these different parts and their functions. With this knowledge, you can operate the camera effectively and get the best output from it.

You're a spirit being but your physical body is a living machine. You didn't have to have a body to exist. The reason you have a body is so you can function for God in this terrestrial plane. The Bible says God gave to every seed its own body (1 Corinthians 15:38), and so, to every human spirit, He gave a human body.

Now, there's a part in this machine (your body) that's so important, and it's your mouth, which houses your tongue. You may have never studied the tongue and its functions, but the Bible, God's manual, enlightens us about it. The Word of God gives us accurate information on the human body, and the functions of its essential members.

Some people think their mouth is meant only for talking, eating, and drinking. These are all lesser uses of the mouth. Some even smoke and curse with it. When you study the Manual (the Bible), you'll discover the most important use of the tongue and the mouth. The primary reason God gave you a mouth is clearly stated in **Joshua 1:8:**

> *"This book of the law shall not depart out of thy mouth; but thou shalt* ***meditate*** *therein day and night, that thou mayest observe to do according to all that is written therein: for then thou shalt make thy way prosperous, and then thou shalt have good success."*

Now the Hebrew word translated "meditate" is "hagah" and it means to mutter or speak under your voice. When you're meditating, it means you're talking or muttering something to yourself.

So when he said, *"Thou shalt meditate,"* he meant *"Thou shall talk the Word under your voice to yourself day and night."* Sometimes it may look like you're soliloquizing. You may just be standing somewhere and talking to yourself. People may look at you funny, thinking something is wrong with you, but that's what it means when the Bible says we are a *peculiar* people. You shouldn't be bothered by what they think or say because you're doing God's Word.

You're using your mouth to create the kind of circumstances you want to have, chart your course, and determine your future.

A Principle From The Beginning

Like every great truth in the Kingdom of God that the Church should learn and walk in, prophesying to your future takes its root from the book of Genesis. When you study from Genesis chapter 1, you'll read,

> *"In the beginning God created the heaven and the earth. And the earth was without form, and void; and darkness was upon the*

> *face of the deep. And the Spirit of God moved upon the face of the waters."*
>
> (Genesis 1:1-2).

Then it shows you something very powerful in the third verse:

> *"And God* said, *Let there be light: and there was light."*

God's beautiful earth had became a chaotic mass, but the Spirit of God began to hover over (or incubate upon) the waters of the earth.

Then God spoke up and *said,* "Let there be light!" and there was light! This was what God did to make the change He wanted—He spoke light into the darkness.

Maybe there's chaos in your life; it could be in your finances, your family, your job, business or academics. The Spirit of God can brood over that situation as you meditate on the Word. Speak to that situation the outcome you want to have and the Spirit of God will swing into action to ensure you have what you say.

You may be a young man, married with little kids, and life doesn't look so good. It looks like life is being unjustly hard on you. Your job or business isn't paying well. You look at your wife and kids and wonder, *"Dear God, what am I going to do?"*

Stop wondering what you're going to do. **I have told you what to do.** Young man, learn to wake up in the night, not to read newspapers or watch movies, but to "talk." When you wake up in the middle of the night, pace the floor and talk to yourself; when you get up in the morning, continue talking. Your family may wonder what you're up to, but you know what you're doing.

The tighter the world pulls its strings and the harder things look, the more you should be talking. Don't let anything frighten you out of your talking. Let me tell you this: the greater the problem, the greater will be its fall before you. The higher the walls of opposition, the greater their fall will be. Satan may keep building his attack against you, but you just keep on talking, and soon enough, his resistance will break and he'll flee from you.

Remember what the Bible says, *"If the clouds be full of rain, they empty themselves upon the earth:"* (Ecclesiastes 11:3). Just keep talking. If you haven't seen the harvest yet, don't stop. Keep talking; the power is in your mouth!

Paul tells us, "Don't ask who will go up to Heaven to bring Christ down, and don't ask who will go down into the deep to bring Him up. The Word is near you, even in your mouth!" (Romans 10:8-10). It's in your mouth! That money you require is in your mouth. That job or business is in your mouth. That pregnancy, that healing you've been waiting for is in your mouth. Glory to God!

Talk More Than You Eat!

You talked yourself to the place you're in right now and you can talk your way forward from here. Your mouth was given to you to say what you want in your life. Stop talking about the things you see in the physical; they won't change that way. Say what you want instead!

When you say what you want, you're functioning rightly and using your mouth for the purpose for which it was designed.

In Romans 10:10 Paul declares that "*With the heart man believeth unto righteousness; and with the mouth confession is made unto salvation.*"

This means that with your mouth, you make the "confessions" (in Greek, this is "Homologia" which means "saying the same things as God") that catapult you into salvation. That's how to enjoy the benefits of righteousness. It's all in your mouth! With your mouth, you catapult yourself into that position that you've seen in your spirit. This is a spiritual principle in the Kingdom of God. If you want to move from point A to point B, you're going to have to talk yourself there. You've got to keep saying it. In fact, you've got to "talk" more than you eat and drink! I told you your mouth wasn't given you just for eating, drinking, and talking to and about other people. Use it to talk your future.

Keep talking and let no one stop you. Keep on declaring who you are in Christ Jesus. You may have been denied promotion or some benefits that were due you in your office. Don't worry. The Bible says promotion doesn't come from the east, west or south; it comes from God (Psalm 75:6). What you're going to do is talk yourself to the top! Use your mouth, for that's where the miracle is.

It may be in the night time or during the day; you may be at work or in your home, it makes no difference; just make sure you're talking.

Prophecies From Years Ago

Many of the great things happening in our ministry today came to us as prophecies many years ago. The Holy Spirit would speak to us and tell us about the days to come and the anointing of God's Spirit that was coming. He'd tell us that we'd preach the gospel in so many places and so many would believe.

We knew these things would happen and we kept talking them for years. That's why they're no surprises at all, at least not to me. We know the reality of that scripture in 1 Corinthians 14:3: "*he that prophesieth* was *speaketh unto men to edification, and exhortation, and comfort."* We were comforted by those prophesies, and today we're living in that comfort of the Holy Ghost that He brought many years ago because we're seeing the reality of those words.

When our ministry was still just beginning, I'd tell our congregation that we're growing the largest Word church in the city. Believe it or not, we're already there. It's the largest Word church in the country.

I remember looking at the National Stadium in Lagos, Nigeria one day and saying, "We're going to use this place for gospel meetings and pack it out." And we did! During the Night of Bliss Special on the 6th of December, 2002, we held the largest gathering ever recorded there with over 500,000 people in attendance. They filled all the grounds, parking space et al. of the stadium complex.

Then again, on the 6th of February, 2004, over 2.5 million people attended a single all-night service that we held in the grounds of the stadium in the city of Port-Harcourt, Nigeria. The mainbowl of the stadium itself one of the several overflow spaces! The prophecies of yesteryears are the realities we're living in today.

Now I've been telling our congregation, "We will network the world." I know what I'm talking about and I really don't care whether or not someone agrees with it. I just keep declaring, "We will network the world," and it's happening already. You see, everybody's got a mouth and it's up to you to say what you want (to have or see) with your own mouth. I said mine and I had what I said and I'm still saying it and it's just as certain that I have what I'm saying now. Praise God forever more!

Chapter Six

WHAT SHOULD YOU DO WITH PROPHECY?

When you hear a word of prophecy that concerns you, you should do what Daniel did. Israel was in captivity and Daniel had been fasting and praying for their freedom. As he studied the scrolls of the Prophet Jeremiah, he found out that the time of Israel's deliverance had come, yet there was no deliverance. So he set himself to pray.

You have to set yourself to pray in order to bring those prophecies into reality. As you pray in the Holy

Ghost, the Spirit of God will guide you into knowing the set time for their fulfilment.

This doesn't mean that the times you pray in the Spirit are the only times He guides you. It just means that your spirit becomes very sensitive and easily picks up signals transmitted from God's frequency at such times. He can let you know, "This is the time for that word!" and when you get that signal, you've got to act, because if you don't act, you may lose it!

Don't say, "Oh God, bring it to pass." No! Understand God's ways. The Psalmist said the children of Israel knew the acts of God but Moses knew the *ways* of God (Psalm 103:7). What I'm teaching right now is one of the ways of God.

Step Into It!

You're the one responsible for bringing about the prophecies in your life.

"How?" you ask.

By stepping into it! Until the priests stepped into the waters of the Jordan, it didn't part. Then again, a stepping into that water at the wrong time and in the wrong way could have gotten them all drowned in the water. But thank God, they stepped in when God said to, and the Jordan parted just as He had prophesied to them.

The prophet said about Jesus, *"Lo, I come: in the volume of the book it is written of me,"* (Psalm 40:7) When Jesus was to step into that, He didn't pray, "O God, you shall make it happen!" He said, "I've come to do thy will, oh God" (Hebrews 10:7).

Look at Him again in Luke chapter 4. He went into the synagogue on the Sabbath day, as was His custom, and was handed the scroll to read. Then He read to the people from where Isaiah stated, *"The Spirit of the Lord is upon me, because he hath anointed me to preach the gospel to the poor; he hath sent me to heal the broken-hearted, to preach deliverance to the captives, and recovering of sight to the blind, to set at liberty them that are bruised, To preach the acceptable year of the Lord"* (Luke 4:18-19).

Afterwards, He closed the book and said to them, "Today, this Scripture is fulfilled in your ears." Right there demon-possessed man screamed out and Jesus said, "Shut up and come out of him!" He put that Word to work immediately and the demon checked out. The people left the synagogue that day amazed at the mighty deed they'd just witnessed (Mark 1:21-28).

Chapter Seven

YOUR TALK IS YOUR FUTURE!

Jesus said to His disciples in Matthew 17:20:

> *"...verily I say unto you, If ye have faith as a grain of mustard seed, ye shall say unto this mountain, Remove hence to yonder place; and it shall remove; and nothing shall be impossible unto you."*

Jesus didn't just speak these fantastic words, He proved them. And these words let you know you're the architect of your life today. Some people don't understand this and they don't believe it, but it doesn't change the fact that it's true. The life you're living today is the exact picture you painted with your words yesterday.

You say, "But this wasn't my plan five years ago." It may not have been your plans, but it was your talk. Your talk is your future. Your tongue is the director of your life. We studied in the book of James and found out how that the tongue is like a captain of a ship. Where your tongue goes, you go. If your tongue is confused, your life will be confused.

Have you ever read about the man Job? Reading his story on the surface, you may come away with the impression that Job was being tested by God. You may even feel that God doesn't really care about His children and can choose to hurt them just to prove a point to the devil. But if you study Job's story carefully, you'll observe that God wasn't the one trying him. God wasn't the one who brought evil upon Job's life. He (Job) brought it upon himself through his words.

Job was responsible for his catastrophe. The devil couldn't inflict those terrible disasters on him until he broke the hedge of protection God had placed around him (Job 1:9-10). It wasn't God who broke that hedge.

Even though he was a wonderful, righteous man who God loved and bragged about, he lived in fear and unbelief. Job said things like, "I'm not safe. I don't know what my children are up to right now. Those kids will be the death of me!"(Job 3:25).

Have you heard people talk like this? And they wonder why their lives are full of ups-and-downs. You have to keep your distance from such people. And if you're like that, you have to change. Otherwise, in a while from now, you will be somewhere you won't like.

I can't tell you this enough: What you have now is the result of what you said years ago. Who you are today is what you said yesterday. You are the picture of what you said yesterday. Your words make you or break you. Don't forget what Proverbs 18:21 says: *"Death and life are in the power of the tongue: and they that love it shall eat the fruit thereof."*

Apart from sin, one thing that's sure to bring sickness or failure to a Christian is "wrong talk." A lot of Christians don't have a problem with sin but with their mouths. In fact, the sin problem they have is the wrong use of their tongue. That's what has put many back into the bondage of sin.

You Are Your Own Responsibility

Why would a man grow and move forward only for his life to suddenly begin to spiral downwards and end up in a ditch. Don't blame it on his family, society, economic forces, or the government. I'm not saying these are not influential, but they can only affect us to the extent that we let them. Your faith and knowledge of the Word will put you over them. The government of any nation should not dictate your prosperity, joy, happiness or success, because these things are not citizens of any particular country.

Assuming you were fired from work, two years ago

you didn't dream you could be fired. You were doing well on the job. You did everything right and to the best of your ability, and yet you were fired. Now you're wondering how you could have been responsible.

Maybe you weren't responsible for getting fired from your job, but you're responsible for staying without one. It's not what you're faced with that's the problem, it's what you do with the situation. Your experience is not the important thing; what really matters is what you do with your experience.

All right, you've been fired, what do you do now? Where do you go from here? Are you looking upward or downward? Do you think it's all over or are you determined to do better and get greater? Where you go from here is what matters, and it's all up to you. Are you going to sit at home and have people come to you and sympathize with you?

When Abraham and Lot were about to separate, Lot chose the best part of the land for himself and left the parched part for Abraham. After he was gone, God spoke to Abraham and asked him to look to the north, south, east, and west; as far as his eyes could see, He had given to him, and that included all the land Lot greedily chose for himself!(Genesis 13:10-17).

Are you going to think and see like Abraham, who God told that as far as his eyes could see was his, or are you going to continue wondering where to start? Yes, you've worked faithfully for that company all these years and you still can't understand why they laid you off. But it's time to quit wondering where you're going to start from. Don't see yourself going down, because if you do, you'll surely go down.

It's time for you to start putting to work the things you've learnt in this book. It's time for you to make your move! Prophesy your future. Locate the Word of God concerning you and speak it out. Speak forth the Word.

Chapter Eight

MAKE YOUR MOVE!

Is there something God has told you to do, or something in your heart you want to achieve? You must make a move! There are things God has declared concerning you; prophecies that have gone forth about your life, but they will not be fulfilled while you're sitting down with folded arms.

Decide today to do something about the dreams and visions that God has given you. As you pray in the Spirit, listen for the guidance of the Holy Ghost within you. As the Spirit ministers back to your spirit, you will be instructed on the particular step to take. When you receive that, you must act.

All You Need Is Within You

Everything you need is inside you. All the capital you need is inside you. When you take a tiny orange seed in your hand, it has all the potentials to produce roots, a stem, branches, leaves and many orange fruits with many seeds in them.

All you need to do is put that little seed in the right environment (the soil) and its potentials will be released. Just like that seed, everything you need to become the "you" that God has destined you to be is inside you.

I say it all the time that I can never fail, I can never be sick or poor. It's impossible; I just can't. I know who I am; I've found my place; I've found my roots!

You say, "Now you're boasting, Pastor Chris."

Yes I am! I'm boasting in God's Word, because I've found out His Word works. The Word of God is living and active. If you put the Word inside you, He'll make you a master over circumstances of life. You will never live in fear or defeat anymore. With the Word inside you, there's no telling how far you'll go. All the limitations will be taken out of your life and your potentialities will be let loose.

Speak Right About Yourself

There's a beautiful prayer of David in Psalm 16 that inspires me so much. David had such insight and revelation of God's purpose for him, and it showed in the way he prayed and prophesied here:

> *"Preserve me, O God: for in thee do I put my trust. O my soul, thou hast said unto the Lord, Thou art my Lord: my goodness extendeth not to thee; But to the saints that are in the earth, and to the ex-*

> *cellent, in whom is all my delight. Their sorrows shall be multiplied that hasten after another god: their drink offerings of blood will I not offer, nor take up their names into my lips. The Lord is the portion of mine inheritance and of my cup: thou maintainest my lot.* ***The lines are fallen unto me in pleasant places; yea, I have a goodly heritage***"
>
> (Psalm 16:1-6).

This is the way to pray. Hold your Bible before you and begin to prophesy these words about your life. Don't ever be cast down. You'll never find me cast down. You say, "Well, Pastor Chris, if I don't ever see you cast down, that doesn't mean you don't get cast down sometimes."

The truth is that I don't get cast down. It's not just because I don't want to (and of course, I don't want to), but more than that, I can't be cast down. You see, I've put God's Word inside me so much that it's just not possible for me to be cast down.

What could it ever be that would make me feel

dejected? I know the lines are fallen unto me in pleasant places, and I have a goodly heritage. I've come to find out what God has done for me. He said He divided the land for an inheritance, and I found out the borders of my land have fallen in the choice parts. He has given me a good land; actually, He gave me the best; Hallelujah!

This is how you should see yourself and talk about your life. Don't say, "My life is so dry, and I'm in this dry place (your office, city, state or country) where nothing happens."

What do you mean, "dry"? Count me out of that portion! As for me, the lines are fallen unto me in pleasant places, and I have a wonderful heritage. It doesn't matter where I find myself; the lines are fallen to me in pleasant places!

David went on to say, *"I will bless the Lord, who hath given me counsel: my reins also instruct me in the night seasons"* (Psalm 16:7). This is what the Lord is doing right now; He's giving you counsel from within. When God gives you counsel you can never be confused. Words like, "I'm so confused; I don't know what to do," wouldn't be found in your vocabulary. Instead of stumbling out of bed in fear because you had a nightmare, your reins (or inner man) would instruct you in the night time.

Like David you should declare, *"I will bless the Lord who counsels me; he gives me wisdom in the night. He tells me what to do"* (Psalm 16:7 TLB).

SEE NOTHING BUT GOD

In the 8th verse of Psalm 16, David said, *"I have set the Lord always before me, because he is at my right hand, I shall not be moved."*

This was David's secret. What have you set before you? What are you looking at? There's an old song we used to sing, but I don't sing it anymore because I discovered we were seeing the wrong thing. Part of that song says, *"When I look to my right, I see satan has fallen; when I look to my left, I see satan has fallen. When I look to my front, I see satan has fallen; when I look to my back, I see satan has fallen. I have seen the downfall of satan, glory be to God."*

My question is: How come it's the fallen devil you're seeing all around you? Where are God and His innumerable company of angels? We know the devil is a fallen foe; he's been defeated already. Now, look and see God; see His glory, beauty, strength, power, grace and favour manifested all around you!

David said, "I have set the Lord always before me." He saw nothing but God, What do you see? I remember the story Kenneth Hagin told of a dear old man of God. He was travelling at sea on a ship, and everyday, throughout the voyage, he would sit up on the deck, looking out to the sea with a faraway look in his eye.

One of the young men who had been observing this strange old man went to him and asked, "Sir, why do you sit out here all by yourself looking out to sea? What do you see out there?"

He replied, "I see nothing but God."

Sitting up on that deck looking out at the vast expanse of the ocean, some other person would have been petrified. Just the thought that you're completely surrounded by water for miles and miles around could be both very humbling and terrifying. But this man didn't see any fear or vulnerability or impending disaster; all he saw was God in all of His glory, power, beauty, and majesty.

Praise God No Matter What

Hezekiah was another man who saw nothing but God. He was on his sickbed when Isaiah, the prophet of God walked into his room and told him to set his house in order for he was surely going to die.

At first, when he heard God's pronouncement from the mouth of the prophet, all he could see was death. He saw himself in the grave; he saw the people crying over his corpse. Then he turned his face to the wall and began to pray, and after a while, all he could see was God.

When he opened his eyes and looked at the world around him, he saw death, but he turned his face to the wall and prayed to the Lord:

> *"I said in the cutting off of my days, I shall*

go to the gates of the grave: I am deprived of the residue of my years. I said, I shall not see the Lord, even the Lord, in the land of the living: I shall behold man no more with the inhabitants of the world....Behold, for peace I had great bitterness: but thou hast in love to my soul delivered it from the pit of corruption: for thou hast cast all my sins behind thy back. For the grave cannot praise thee, death can not celebrate thee: they that go down into the pit cannot hope for thy truth. The living, the living, he shall praise thee, as I do this day: the father to the children shall make known thy truth. The Lord was ready to save me: therefore we will sing my songs to the stringed instruments all the days of our life in the house of the Lord"

(Isaiah 38:10-11;17-20).

He kept on talking to God like this and prophesying God's Word back to Him. And before Isaiah could make it out into the middle court of the palace, God stopped him in his tracks and said to him, "I have rescinded that decision. Go back to Hezekiah and tell him I've heard his prayer. He's not going to die; not only have I healed him, I've also added fifteen more years to his life"(Isaiah 38:4-5).

Begin To Prophesy!

Child of God, this is how to pray! Don't stay there whining, "I don't know why I didn't get the job. After all, I was more qualified than the others. This bad luck has followed me for so many years."

What do you mean bad luck? Prophesy about your future and declare: *"I don't know any bad luck. The Bible declares that all things work together for good to them that love God, to them who are the called according to His purpose. I love God and He has called me according to His divine purpose. Therefore, everything is working out for my good, in the Name of Jesus!"*

Don't you dare give up on the visions God has shown you. Straighten up, square your shoulders, chest out, chin up, and elbow the devil out of your way!

Push your way through every obstacle as you speak words of power. The walls will crumble before you and the seas will divide, and you will go through victoriously!

Now that you've found out you can prophesy about your future, it's time to make your move. It's time to prophesy! Prophesy about your life and your future; talk the Word about your ministry, your body, your family, your job, your finances, your country, and everything that concerns you.

See your progress instead of stagnation, and declare these words with all boldness and authority:

> *"I refuse to fear. I see things changing for the best. I am fully persuaded that my God is able to perform that which He has spoken concerning me. Therefore I refuse to stagger at His Word, and I remain strong in faith, giving glory to God. My health is blossoming; my finances are increasing. I see my progress. I see my prosperity. I see my promotion. I see it! Glory to God!*

> *Greater is He that is in me than he that is in the world. I have the ability of God in me. I can do all things through Christ which strengthens me. The anointing is upon me, causing me to make progress and move forward. I'm getting better, stronger and greater by the day. I'm walking in victory, in the Name of Jesus Christ!*

Open your mouth now and speak words of faith and power. Prophesy the Word of God to your life everyday and to your future, and watch it come to pass. Glory to God!

To contact the author write:

Pastor Chris Oyakhilome:

United Kingdom:
Christ Embassy Int'l office
363 Springfield Road
Chelmsford, Essex, CM2 6AW
Tel:+44 1245 490 234

Please include your testimony or help received from this book when you write. Your prayer requests are welcome.

South Africa:
303 Pretoria Avenue
Cnr.Harley and Hendrik Vewoerd,
Randburg, Gauteng, South Africa.
Tel:+27 72 241 7332

Nigeria:
Christ Embassy
P.O. Box 13563, Ikeja,
Lagos, Nigeria.
Tel:+234-802 332 4187-9;
+234-1-773 7611-5

or email:pastorchris@christembassy.org

NEW RELEASE BY
PASTOR CHRIS

Catch a passion for prayer as you discover the dynamic principles of effective prayer in this book. The principles are simple, the results are guaranteed - a life full of joy and peace as you receive answers to your prayers ... always!

To know more about the ministry and messages of Pastors Chris & Anita Oyakhilome contact:

CHRIST EMBASSY

aka Believers' LoveWorld Inc.

LONDON:
Christ Embassy Int'l Office

363 Springfield Road
Chelmsford, Essex, CM2 6AW
Tel:+44 1245 490 234

SOUTH AFRICA:
Cnr. Harley and Hendrik Veword
Randburg, Gauteng.
South Africa.
Tel: +27-72-241 7332

NIGERIA:
P.O. Box 13563, Ikeja,
Lagos, Nigeria.
Tel: +234 - 802 3324 188,
+234 - 805 2464 131,
+234 - 1 - 892 5724

email: cec@christembassy.org
website: www.christembassy.org